THE LIFE OF
BENEDICT XVI
FOR YOUNG READERS

Claire Jordan Mohan

Illustrations

Jane Robbins

New Hope Publications
New Hope, KY

Mohan, Claire Jordan
The Life of Benedict XVI for Young Readers

SUMMARY: Describes the young life of Joseph Cardinal Ratzinger
of Germany, focusing on his boyhood years and young manhood.
Also details the politics, history and religion which influenced him.
Included are his interests, pastimes, and a discussion of the many
obstacles he faced as a child and young man. Clearly written, factual
story.

1. Benedict XVI. Pope. 1927- . Juvenile literature.
2. Popes—Biography—Juvenile literature.
Benedict XVI. Pope. 1927- . 1. Title [B] [92] 2. Popes.

Cover photo: Grzegorz Galazka

ISBN #978-1-892875-40-2

CONTENTS

To my dear husband, Bob,
who always knew the true meaning of the word "love."

COAT OF ARMS

(See in color on back cover of this book)

The coat of arms consists of a shield bearing several important symbols. Pope Benedict XVI's shield is principally red. In each upper corner there is a *chape* (cape), a symbol of religion.

At the point of honor is a large gold scallop shell which has a triple symbolism: one, that the limited mind cannot take in the infinity of God; two, it is a symbol of a pilgrim; and three, it is an emblem found in the coat of arms of the monastery near Regensburg to which Joseph Ratzinger feels spiritually closely bound.

In the corner to the left is a Moor's head. This is the ancient symbol of the diocese of Freising of which Benedict was archbishop.

In the opposite corner of the shield, a brown bear is portrayed with a pack-saddle on its back. This is the symbol of a bear which, according to a story, was tamed by God's grace. The bear is the bishop of Freising himself; the pack-saddle is the burden of his episcopate.

At the top is the papal miter (hat) with three bands of gold joined at the center to show their unity in the same person.

The gold-fringed pallium stands for the pope's responsibility as pastor of the flock entrusted to him by Christ, and a symbol of the pope's brotherly love for his bishops.

The crossed keys, one gold and the other silver, are symbols of spiritual and temporal power. They signify the power that Christ gave to St. Peter and his successors.

A *cartouche*, or ribbon, is often used below the shield to place the pope's motto. The absence of a motto in Pope Benedict's coat of arms implies openness without exclusion to all ideals that may derive from faith, hope, and charity.

*"May Christ always take first place
in our thoughts and actions."*

CHAPTER 1

THE BEGINNING

◆ ◆ ◆

Snow covered the ground and swirled in the cold freezing wind in Germany on April 16, 1927, the day before Easter. There was no thought of pretty hats or shiny shoes. No colored eggs or baskets of goodies were hidden for the children in the Ratzinger home. They were not waiting for the Easter bunny, but they were waiting for something…they just didn't know what it was.

Papa had said, "Now, you two, be very quiet," as he and their neighbor ran up the stairs to the second floor. His blonde hair was uncombed and his usually neat shirt tails trailed out of his pants. He had not gone to work, and Mama was still resting in bed. Puzzled, the children wondered why the neighbor lady was upstairs with them.

Two-year-old Georg couldn't sit still. He ran to the steps and called, "Mama! Mama!" His little wooden wagon and building blocks lay untouched in the parlor as he toddled back to the kitchen and pulled at his sister's arm.

Five-year-old Maria ignored him as she huddled by the wood stove, quietly drinking a mug of warm milk. For a while, she watched the flames flicker and the logs glow, listening to her brother's pleas. Then she got off her stool to look out the window. The snowflakes were falling on the sill. There were drifts by the back door. Georg was starting to cry.

"Come here, Georg," she called as she put her small arms out to him. The wind outside howled and there were strange sounds from the upstairs bedroom...there was a whimper. It sounded like a puppy.

"Maria, what's that?" Georg questioned her. She hugged him, but she could only answer, "It's okay, Georg," because she herself was puzzled.

Within minutes their father called down to them. "Maria, Georg, come up here." Obediently, Maria took Georg's hand and they dashed up the steps.

The bedroom seemed dark. The snow clouded the window. They saw their mother lying against her pillows holding something. They heard a little cry and saw that it was a *baby* in their mother's arms—two tiny blue eyes gazed at them. They stared in disbelief.

"Maria, Georg, you have a new little brother," Mama told them. They reached out and touched the little red face. Mama smiled.

"What do you think of this little fellow?" she asked as she put her arms around them. "This is Joseph. He just came from Heaven. Isn't he sweet?" Patting their heads, she added, "You can help me take care of him."

They touched the fuzzy blonde head gently. They reached for the tiny fingers and then nuzzled close to their mother.

Papa kissed Mama's cheek as he knelt by the bed and held her hand. "We must thank God for this treasure," he said. He started to pray. Georg and Maria clasped their little hands and joined their parents.

When they had finished, Mama looked at the window frosted with snowflakes and turned to Papa.

"Dear," she said, "it looks like it is getting worse outside. I am very tired and sleepy now, but you must hurry to take little Joseph to the church and have the priest baptize him."

It was the custom of the time. Papa knew this, so he carefully lifted the baby from her arms and wrapped him in the soft blue afghan which lay on the rocking chair by the bureau. As he did this, the children remembered that just last week they had seen Mama sitting by the fire knitting something blue and fluffy.

Papa and the children went downstairs where Maria ran to the closet and grabbed their coats. Georg reached for his favorite red hat and mittens. As Papa put on his dark woolen overcoat and pulled his hat down over his ears, Maria tugged at his hand.

"Papa, we'll go with you," she announced.

"Oh, no, little one, you can't come. You must stay with Mama."

"Please, Papa," pleaded Maria, "I'll be good."

"I'm sorry, love," he told her, patting her blonde curls. "It is snowing hard and we can't have you catching a cold."

Maria's eyes watered and tears spilled down her cheeks. She wanted to be with her father and her new brother. She wanted to know what "baptize" meant, but Father grabbed another warm shawl from the closet and tucked the baby close to him.

Shivering, he closed the door and met the swirling flakes, his brown boots pushing holes into the deep snow. He stopped at the home of the godparents, and together they braved the cold wind as they made their way to the nearby rectory. The priest joined them and they all hurried to the church. The doors were open and the baptismal water was ready. "Joseph Aloysius" was baptized.

It was Holy Saturday, the feast of St. Benedict Joseph Labre, who was called "the Beggar of Rome." No one thought much about it at the time, but years later this name would have special meaning to many people in the world.

CHAPTER 2

EARLY YEARS

◆ ◆ ◆

Though the new baby's grandparents were farmers, his father had chosen a far different way of life. Joseph was a rural police officer who fell in love with and married a beautiful young girl who cooked at the various hotels in their area. Her name was Maria. Both Joseph and Maria were very holy people who went to Mass often during the week and sometimes three times on Sunday! They loved God and taught their children to be close to Him.

Life in Germany the year Baby Joseph was born was not easy for many people. There was much unemployment, and there were political problems, restlessness, and many illnesses throughout the country. Still, little Joseph and his brother and sister had a happy life with parents who loved them. His father had a steady job, and at that time these issues did not affect them.

Once he started to toddle, Joseph and his brother were always doing things together. Georg, now the "big brother," was more daring and outgoing. He led his shy younger brother through many adventures.

As with some children today, it seemed the Ratzingers were always moving because of their father's job. When Joseph was two, the family left the village of Marktl am Inn where he had been born and moved to Tittmoning, a small town on the Salzach River. It was a wonderful place. There was a majestic town square with a sparkling fountain.

Joseph lived in the most beautiful house on the town square, which combined the police station with their home. It was a house full of mystery and excitement. Though the outside was beautiful, the inside was a different story—the floor was full of cracks, the stairs were steep and the rooms were crooked. The kitchen and living room were narrow and the bedrooms uncomfortable. Though cooking and cleaning such a house was hard on their mother, to the children it was a wonderful place. The boys especially loved to play games running around the house and hiding in all the nooks and crannies.

Though the two brothers had fun on their own, they loved it when their mother would take them on long hikes through the woods nearby. Their little legs grew strong as they climbed to the top of the hill that rose to a little chapel. Trees and brambles were everywhere. They would stop and pray, then run about, hiding from each other in the bushes. Nearby you could hear the clear waters of a brook rushing down to the valley. It seemed to sing as it ran by. While Georg liked to trip on the rocks, little Joseph would toss stones into the sparkling stream and cup his hands to drink the cool mountain water.

"Are you tired?" Mama asked every time.

"Oh, no, Mama, we want to see the fort!" they would answer in unison. Mama held their hands as they climbed over the uneven ground until they came to a mighty fortress that towered over the nearby town. Joseph was fascinated by it.

"Mama, tell us the story," he begged as soon as it came into his sight.

"Let's sit here by the rocks," said his mother as she spread her shawl on the soft green grass. Joseph curled close, leaning his head on her shoulder.

"Once upon a time…," she began. Though Joseph had heard the tale many times, the words, like soft music, were always new to him. He never tired of listening.

During the Christmas season they would walk through the village and gaze at the shop windows that were illuminated at night with bright lights. Georg, with little Joseph clutching his hand, would wander around the town looking at the nativity scenes.

"Georg, look at Mary and Joseph and all the shepherds. Someday, when I get big, I will carve like that. I will make the Baby Jesus so beautiful," little Joseph would say. Mama had told him the story of the first Christmas, and little Joseph responded with a kind and tender heart, saying, "If Jesus were here now, we could take him to our house. We would never say 'no room' to him, would we, Georg?"

"Of course not. Mama and Papa would set up our little crib for him," replied his brother.

"And Mary and Joseph could sleep in my bed," added Joseph.

During the fall, as they walked through the fields, Mama showed them how to find many things to build their own manger. Often she would take them to visit an elderly lady who had a nativity scene that almost filled her whole living room. It held so many wonderful things and looked so real. When Mama called, "Come, children," they were never ready to leave.

"Just one more minute, Mama," Joseph would plead. "Mama, I want to see the shepherds."

"Ah, yes, my son, I will wait just one more minute, then you must get home to bed."

Whether it was the Baby Jesus or the dying Jesus, little Joseph's heart was always touched.

At Easter time Joseph worried about the crucified Jesus. His mother told him how cruelly Jesus had been treated. With tears in his eyes, he would wonder how anyone would want to hurt the Lord.

"I would fight those bad men," Joseph said to his mother as he bravely swung his arms.

The young parents would smile and be happy that already the children loved Jesus and cared so much. They taught Maria, Georg, and Joseph to be good, to have courage and to persevere in whatever they did. Even when the children were little, their papa taught them to think about things and to understand right from wrong.

CHAPTER 3

THE HITLER YOUTH

◆ ◆ ◆

In 1932, when Joseph was five, the family moved again. This time his mother had a modern house without creaking, uneven floors or nooks and crannies. It became a cozy home. The police offices were on the first floor and the Ratzingers lived on the second floor. Outside there was a garden, and there was a large meadow nearby. The children would run around happily and play hide-and-seek in the tall grass.

One day Mama was in the kitchen baking bread. She heard a scream.

"Mama, Mama, come quick!" called Maria.

Mama threw the dough onto the counter and ran down the steps and out the door. She flew across the grass. Joseph was splashing frantically in the water of a nearby pond. Maria and Georg were trying to reach him, but the water was too deep and they were in danger, too. Fully clothed, Mama jumped into the water, grabbed Joseph in her arms and pulled the other two to the shore. She hugged her littlest son tight, and carried the boy back to the house.

"Joseph, you must never *ever* go near that water again!" she said as she sat with him on the porch step, wrapping him in a fuzzy towel that Maria had gotten from the apartment. "You could have drowned. Then what would Mama do without you?"

Joseph was happy to be safe in his mother's arms. He stopped crying and kissed her.

"I love you, Mama," he said, then explained, "…but Mama, I was just trying to catch a fish for dinner."

On January 30, 1933, Adolf Hitler became the chancellor of Germany. Joseph's older brother and sister, Maria and Georg, attended school where they were taught about National Socialism. Though they didn't understand what that meant, they had often heard their father say that the new government officials were criminals.

One rainy day in January, the principal entered the classroom and interrupted their work.

"Children, line up," the teachers ordered. "We will have a parade throughout the village to celebrate our new *Führer*, our new leader."

The boys and girls put down their books and marched outside. It was cold and damp, and the ground was slushy, but the children tramped throughout the village until they were finally told to go home. That night, Maria and Georg asked their father, "Why?"

Something was happening in Germany. Life was changing for everyone. At first the schoolteachers continued to teach Bible class, but the schools' foundation was no longer to be the Christian faith but the ideology of the *Führer*. Soon there were new teachers.

Many members of the Nazi Party were in the town. They brought out uniforms for the children to wear. The boys were encouraged to join the "Hitler Youth" and the girls, the "League of German Girls." They were told they must be "swift as a greyhound, tough as leather, and hard as steel." This was to be the motto of every German child.

It was the goal of the Nazis to persuade every qualified boy or girl to be part of this group. Later on, all who qualified would be required to join. This would include Joseph and his brother and sister. Resistance would have been disastrous. However, not every boy and girl qualified. They had to have racial purity. They could not have any Jewish ancestors, nor could they be of African, Chinese, Polish, or Indian descent. There could be no hereditary diseases in their family — and they had to be physically fit.

The children joined when they were as young as four years of age. By the age of ten they were all members of the Hitler Youth. By fourteen the boys had many choices for service, such as aviation, mechanics, and equestrian duties.

The girls' choices were fewer. Their purpose was to have genetically and racially pure and healthy children. They were prepared to be good strong mothers of the future soldiers of the German race. Hitler told the boys and girls that Germany's future was in their hands. The children felt this was a noble goal.

The boys and girls proudly wore uniforms. The boys wore heavy black shoes with short black stockings, black shorts, a brown shirt with a *swastika* armband, and a cap. They wore various insignia depending on the group to which they belonged. The girls wore heavy marching shoes, stockings, full blue skirts, white blouses, and cotton neckerchiefs with wooden rings bearing the group insignia. For bad weather the girls had heavy blue training suits, slacks and capes. All of the children went through an initiation ceremony and swore an oath to Adolf Hitler. He was soon to be their god.

All other youth groups were banned, including sport and church groups. Children who wanted to be part of a club had no choice but to join the Hitler Youth Group. This group did offer many fun and exciting activities. There was the drill, but also hiking, camping, war games, and sports. The boys and girls were taught that their first loyalty was to the state instead of to the family. Sometimes parents were reported by their own children for disloyal behavior.

When Joseph and his brother and sister questioned their father about these things, he tried to explain to them what was happening.

"My children, Hitler is an evil man. We are all in danger. Our Jewish friends are being punished. Some people are spying and informing on priests. They call them 'enemies of the *Reich*.' I warn them, but there is only so much that I can do. These are not good times. We must stay close to each other and to Jesus," he replied.

One day, Joseph was out playing with his friends in the forest. He noticed something unusual. He reported this to his father.

"Papa, I think there is a factory hidden in the woods."

"Ah, Joseph, there are many strange things happening. Do you not see the lighthouse out on the hill? Did you not see the light flashing in the sky at night? They tell us it is to search for enemy planes."

"But, Papa, I never see any planes in the sky."

"That is true, son, that is true," the father replied. "You are just a little boy, but you are trying understand things. I am proud of you. Things will get better. We must all pray every day for our country."

His father, a wise man, wanted no part of all this. He knew that a victory for Hitler would not be a victory for Germany.

CHAPTER 4

NEW EDUCATION

◆ ◆ ◆

Things did not get better, for no one could ignore the political murmurings and the movement of the troops. Yet, for a while, the Ratzinger family's life remained basically unchanged. Joseph turned six and started school. He felt important walking there with his brother and sister. Their little school still had crucifixes in every classroom. The children still prayed at the beginning and close of each day.

"Mama, I love school," said Joseph one day as he came running into his back yard after class. "Today I learned so much." His mother was carefully taking the clothes off the line and folding them. She placed a clothespin in her basket and turned to her son, putting her arm around him.

"Come, tell me all about it," she said as they went to sit on the stone doorstep.

"Mama," he said excitedly, "look at my book! I'm learning to read, and I'm even studying Latin just like the altar boys at church."

Soon, however, things changed at Joseph's school. Hitler Youth activities interrupted the day. Though not everyone had been forced to join the groups yet, the children who were members proudly left class while the others had to continue their studies. Teachers were required to let them leave without any make-up work or homework. Classical languages were forgotten and English was taught to every grade. Religion was eliminated.

Mr. Ratzinger watched his country fall apart. He was concerned about his children, but he knew that interference with a child's desire to join the Hitler Youth, or openly disagreeing with Nazi ideology in front of a son or daughter, could result in serious consequences for parents. Hitler warned that if parents did anything to discourage their children, the Nazis would take the children away from them. Parents were told that "the lives of all German youths belong solely to Hitler."

Around this time, night shifts and the stress of the political situation caused Joseph's father to become sick and leave his job—but to little Joseph it was wonderful to have his father home with him.

"Let's go for a hike, boys," his father would often call to them. Joseph and Georg would run through the woods, playing games and listening to the tales their father told.

"Tell us about when you were a boy, Papa," Joseph would say.

"Well, now, let me see…" Papa would answer, and they would learn of a simpler world when days had been happier.

Finally, on March 6, 1937, Mr. Ratzinger turned sixty and retired from the police force. A few years before, he had bought an old house out in the country which he had fixed up. There was a loft, and there were roomy sheds as well, and all kinds of other things to fascinate two active boys.

One evening after supper, Papa made a decision. As he and his wife sat on the sofa in the sitting room, he suddenly placed his *stein* of beer on the nearby table and turned to his wife.

"Maria, I think we should move soon. I don't like what is happening here. The country house will be a better place for Maria, Georg, and Joseph. We will be far away from all this turmoil," he said as he tossed the newspaper to the floor.

Mama smiled. "Oh, Joseph, I know that will be good for the children. Let's do it right away," she replied.

They told Maria, Georg, and Joseph the news the next morning. Before long, the Ratzinger family put all their affairs in order, packed up their furniture and all their possessions in a truck, hopped into a borrowed car, and headed to their new home.

The first thing ten-year-old Joseph saw were cherry, plum, pear, and apple trees filled with blossoms. He broke off a flowering branch and gave it to his mother. She held it close to her heart. He climbed a tall oak tree while noticing a pine forest just beyond, waiting to be explored. On the other side a meadow was filled with bright primroses.

Joseph ran to give his father a hug. "Oh, Papa, thank you!" he exclaimed. "I love it here. I think it is like Heaven!"

A few days later, classes at his school, called the Gymnasium for Classical Languages, began. So far this school, not yet under the Nazi influence, did not place as much stress on physical activities. Joseph's exercise came when he had to walk about a half hour each day to reach school. Georg and Maria would rush ahead, but Joseph was the sort of boy who loved peace and quiet. Happily, he would listen to the birds, search for rabbits, and think to himself.

Though he was the youngest and smallest boy in the class, Joseph excelled. One day the teacher told his mother, "You can be proud of this little boy. He does well in all his subjects and he is eager to learn." Maria thanked her and hurried home to tell her husband.

For a while, Latin, which Joseph still enjoyed, was taught, but a year later all this changed. Latin and Greek were gone, replaced by English and natural science. Soon religion was banned in this school, too. Crucifixes were removed from the classrooms. Physical education and sports became the main focus. Teachers and coaches were Nazi sympathizers. Hitler's plans for education had reached even this country school!

For a while Joseph and his brother were altar boys and members of the Catholic youth group, but soon they had less and less time for that as they, too, because of their racial purity, were ordered to join the Hitler Youth Group. When the "Law Concerning the Hitler Youth" was passed, it was legally mandated that every boy and girl of "pure German blood" must join. There could be no resistance or disagreement with the Nazis. To resist was considered treason. Anyone who was opposed risked arrest, jail, or death.

Hitler wanted his young people to be strong in body and was less concerned about the mind and the spirit. Physical education was more important. Of course, at first, most of the children did not mind this, but Joseph's parents were concerned. They knew that Hitler felt that "he who controls the youth controls the future." To many of the youth of that day, Hitler was the new god.

At home, the spiritual education of the Ratzingers did not diminish. Mass, morning and evening prayer, and the daily rosary were ever a part of their lives. The children were taught to be kind and caring, but they could not defy the law. They had no choice.

For a time, the family was able to travel to nearby Austria where they prayed in the beautiful churches. Afterward, they could even attend the famous Salzburg music festivals, where they listened to the boys' choir and learned to love the music of Beethoven and Mozart.

In school, though, instead of praying to or thanking a Christian God, the children were praying to the National Socialist state and to the *Führer*. In these prayers, it was Hitler, not Christ, who was the savior. Children were often required to say this prayer to receive their free lunch:

> Führer, my Führer, bequeathed to me by the Lord,
> Protect and preserve me as long as I live!
> Thou hast rescued Germany from deepest distress,
> I thank thee today for my daily bread.
> Abideth thou long with me,
> forsaketh me not, Führer, my Führer,
> my faith and my light!
> *Heil, mein Führer.*

CHAPTER 5

A NEW DIRECTION

◆ ◆ ◆

One sunny morning after Joseph had carefully extinguished the candles following Sunday Mass, his pastor took him aside.

"My son," he said as he patted him on the head, "you are a good boy and a serious student. I would like to see you enter the minor seminary like your brother Georg. I think you might make a fine priest someday." Then in a husky voice he continued, "For now, the seminary would not only give you a better education, but you would also be free from the Nazi influence."

Joseph looked at the priest and nodded his head.

"Well, Father, Georg has told me so much about his life there. I know I would like it, but I'll have to see what my parents have to say," he replied.

At the supper table that night, Joseph told his parents what the pastor had said. His father smiled at his mother, pleased with the idea, but then he shook his head.

"Ah, Joseph, that sounds good," he answered as he looked across the table at Mama. "I wish I could say yes, but we couldn't afford it. We are already paying for Georg. My pension is too small for both of you."

As she reached for a handkerchief to wipe her eyes, his mother continued, "We really would love you to be a priest, Joseph. You know that, but there's no way for Papa to handle it right now."

His sister Maria put down her fork and quickly looked up from her plate of Mama's garden vegetables. She turned to her father. "Papa, don't worry. I am making good money now that I have graduated. I'll help out. Joseph must go to the seminary!" she cried as she reached out to hug her brother.

And so the next day, Joseph relayed the good news to his pastor, who made the arrangements. He could hardly wait to go. He had heard so much about life at the seminary.

But Joseph, still a shy boy of twelve, was not like his outgoing brother. After a few weeks he came home for a weekend visit. As they sat at the kitchen table drinking from their mugs, his parents questioned him about his life at the seminary — and they were troubled by his answers.

"Joseph, you don't look happy. What's wrong?"

"Mama, I don't like life at the boarding school. It's not for me. For one, you know how I am used to studying quietly by myself, alone in my room whenever I wish. Now I have to study in a large hall, surrounded by sixty other boys, at a certain time each day. I just can't work that way."

"Oh, Joseph, just be patient. Things will work out," he was told.

"But, Papa, I've always been a good student, but now my marks are down. I'm trying my best, but nothing is the way I had expected. I don't know what to do."

They could see that he was close to tears. Lovingly, they both put their arms around him.

"Just wait a bit, son, and see what happens," they told him. "Come, let's go into the parlor." They sat on the sofa and listened kindly as he continued with the rest of his story.

Joseph was very smart, but because of the new progressive ways of the Hitler regime, the boys in all schools, even those in the seminary, spent less time on their studies. They had to play sports for at least two hours every day. This was torture for him.

Joseph was the youngest boy there. He was not muscular or strong like his brother, and he was not up to all that physical activity. He knew he was not good in sports, and that upset him. Though he tried his best to keep up, he was always the last to be chosen no matter what the game. Most of the other boys tried to include him, but he knew they only did it to be kind.

"We know it is hard on you, Joseph. Don't worry about being like the others. You just have to be yourself. Things will get better. You'll see. Just keep trying for a little longer. God will help you," he was told...so he did not quit.

Soon life changed even in the seminary. The war, which broke out in September 1939, appeared almost unreal. After Hitler had brutally brought down Poland, things became quiet. Then in 1940 Denmark and Norway were occupied; Holland, Belgium, Luxembourg and France were brought to their knees. The Balkans came next, and an invasion of Britain was planned.

Huge transports began to roll into the village, bringing home horribly wounded soldiers. The seminary was turned into a military hospital and the students were sent back home to their old schools. Joseph was nearly fourteen, but Georg, who was now seventeen, was drafted into the army.

Eventually, a former convent was found suitable for the seminary, and Joseph returned to his studies. This time, there was no space for a sports field, but there were still outdoors activities. The boys took group hikes, built dams, and caught fish. This was more to Joseph's liking. It required thinking, but not great stamina and strength. Joseph learned to be more sociable as he was happily accepted for himself.

Soon life changed again for the students. It was hard to study. There was sadness throughout the school. Each day the newspapers listed the names of young men who had died in the war—many were boys who had been their classmates. Almost every day there was a funeral Mass. So many wounded soldiers were brought home from the front that eventually the new seminary was also turned into a hospital, and Joseph was sent home for good.

Back in his old school, the students were encouraged by their teachers to be heroes. They were urged to love and even die for their country. His teacher told them, "Don't worry, boys, only one soldier in a thousand will be killed." But this was not true. As Germany lost more men, younger and younger boys and girls, some as young as twelve, were called to serve. Boys who dreamed of winning medals for bravery were faced with the actual brutality of war. In the Battle of Berlin alone, a total of 5,000 Hitler Youth were involved...and only 500 survived!

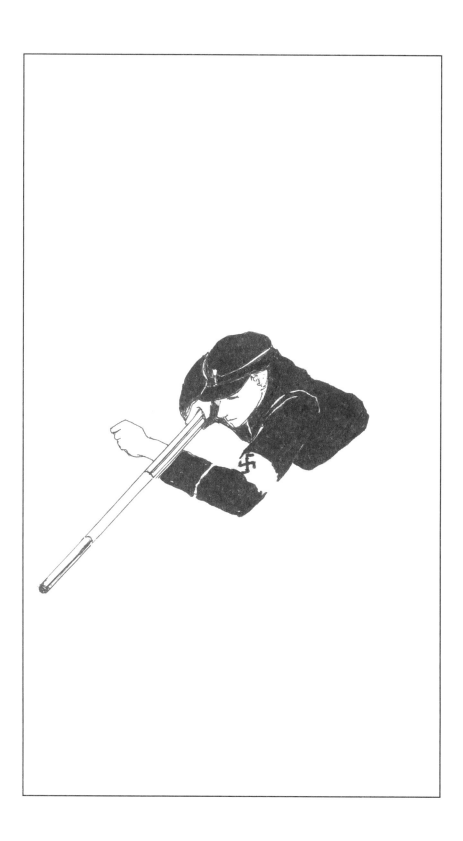

CHAPTER 6

SERVING HIS COUNTRY

◆ ◆ ◆

In 1943, it was decided that boys in boarding schools would be sent to places where they could help in the war effort. They were moved into barracks with regular soldiers, given uniforms and assigned military duties to help defend the city of Munich. The Allied planes were dropping bombs on the city. The bombers soared through the sky day and night on the way to their mission, unaware that down below, teenage boys were aiming to blow them out of the sky, while even younger boys were manning the searchlights to help them. Other young people had been organized to assist families that had been hurt or had lost their homes in the bombings.

Joseph, who was sixteen now, and his fellow seminarians were forced to join this effort. They were sent as a group to several military posts. Many young boys dreamed of being heroes—dying for Hitler. Joseph and the other seminarians did not share this dream. But many of their friends did lose their lives.

In the midst of all this chaos, the boys were expected to continue with their schooling. Teachers came out to the firing positions and held twenty-two hours of classroom instruction a week, literally between the guns.

After a while, Joseph was transferred to telephone communications and was exempt from all military exercises. He even had a room of his own, and when he finished his hours of service, he could do whatever he wanted. He and several other boys were allowed to take the train to Munich where they attended classes three times a week.

The sight of all the destruction around them was frightening. They could see the city slowly falling into ruins—homes and churches were being destroyed. There was chaos everywhere. Finally...there were no trains. Eventually every school throughout all of Germany was closed.

On September 10, 1944, when he was seventeen, Joseph was drafted into the regular army, where he worked with the labor detail erecting tank blockades and trenches. Life here was much harder on the boys. Part of the work also included coming into contact with people from the Dachau concentration camp. Joseph never forgot the suffering faces and the mistreatment he saw...though, as a young soldier, he was helpless to change it.

At the same time, fanatical SS officers attempted to recruit the young soldiers, intimidating them in the middle of the night. The SS was made up of only the best, racially pure Nazis. The SS, or *Schutztaffel*, German for "protective echelon," started as a small personal bodyguard for Hitler, headed by Heinrich Himmler. It later became a huge organization that ran concentration camps and carried out mass executions of political opponents, Jews, gypsies, Polish leaders, Communists, anti-Nazi guerrillas, and Soviet POWs. It gained a reputation as a group of fanatical fighters. To be chosen was considered an honor, but to be part of this, a young man would have to renounce his religion. Nazism was the SS religion and Hitler was their god. Many of Joseph's friends were forced into this cruel group.

Though he was frightened when questioned and pressured by the SS officers, Joseph bravely told them, "I am from the seminary and I intend to become a Catholic priest."

The officer laughed. "You are a fool!" he said. "There is no need for priests to deceive us. There is no God."

Like Jesus, this young boy and his friends were mocked and verbally abused, but Joseph didn't mind because he was spared from serving in the SS, where the officers were known for their harsh treatment of the helpless in the concentration camps. Joseph told his friends, "I have seen some Jews being cruelly treated and others being loaded onto trains and shipped off to certain death. How could we bear to be part of that?"

Many months passed as the boys labored building blockades and trenches. The Americans were advancing, but Joseph's regiment was not called to the front.

On April 30, 1945, word came that Hitler had shot himself, and there was hope that the war would soon end.

In May Joseph decided to desert the army. He wanted to go home. He had had enough of war. This meant that he would now be considered an enemy of the Third Reich! He knew that if he were caught, he would be executed on the spot or hung from a lamp post or a tree by the SS troops as a lesson for others. Still, his heart told him to take a chance.

The city was surrounded by soldiers who had orders to shoot deserters on sight. Fortunately, Joseph was familiar with the area and headed for a little-known back road. He was approached by two soldiers as he walked out of a railroad underpass. His heart stopped beating when he saw them, but they, too, had had enough of war. They needed to find an excuse to let him pass.

"Wait," said one, "he has his arm in a sling. He is wounded. Let him go."

The other soldier gave him a push and said, "Comrade, move on."

Finally, Joseph arrived home.

"Joseph, my son!" cried his mother with tears streaming down her cheeks. His father was speechless as he put his arms around his boy.

But the Americans soon arrived in the village. When Joseph was identified as a soldier, he was taken prisoner, forced to put on the uniform he hated, and marched to a prisoner-of-war camp. Along with about fifty thousand others, he lived outdoors with only a ladleful of soup and a little bread each day for about a month until June 19, 1945, when he was finally released. The soldiers boarded a truck to Munich and found their own way home at last.

Just before sunset three days later, Joseph arrived back in his village. He heard praying and singing coming from the church as he passed by, and wondered if his family was in there praying for him. He didn't stop to find out as he rushed to his home as fast as he could.

When he opened the door, he saw his father sitting in the kitchen. "Papa!" he called.

Mr. Ratzinger looked up at the sound of his son's voice. "Joseph, Joseph, you are safe," he kept repeating.

His mother and sister had heard the news from a neighbor as they were returning from the services. They ran to embrace him. "Oh, my son, at last you are home for good!" cried his mother. She couldn't stop holding him. Finally, she let him go.

"Sit down and rest, Joseph. You must be starving. Ah, Mama will make something special," she added as she hurried to the garden to pick some vegetables.

After assuring them that he really was home safely, Joseph asked his parents about his brother. His mother started to weep as his father answered.

"Joseph, we are so happy you're home, but we don't know what has happened to Georg." Papa took off his glasses and wiped his eyes. "We haven't heard from him for over a month and we worry that he might have been wounded or killed by the American troops."

Mama raised her eyes to Heaven and added, "Oh, Joseph, we pray every minute that God will protect him, but it is all so hard on Papa and me."

Two weeks later, on a sunny morning, just as they had finished saying their morning prayers, the door opened and in walked Georg. Papa, Mama, Maria, and Joseph all jumped from their chairs and grabbed him. Georg, as tearful as they were, held them close for a long while; then, he sat down at his beloved piano and played, "Holy God, We Praise Thy Name…" They held hands as together they sang the words.

Though their world had changed and many of their friends and neighbors had fallen in the war, the Ratzinger family was all together once again.

CHAPTER 7

NEW BEGINNINGS

◆ ◆ ◆

During the long years of Hitler's regime, Mr. Ratzinger had been sadly aware that things were not right in his homeland—even though he had to live with it. He and his wife often discussed this at home, and their religious fervor had kept Maria, Georg and Joseph faithful to their God.

Other young people who had been raised to worship Hitler were left with a defeated Germany and a dead leader. Their god was gone, the Hitler Youth that had shaped their lives was gone, and a whole generation of betrayed children became aware of the unbelievable atrocities committed by their leaders. For them, the years ahead would be difficult.

Joseph and Georg were among the fortunate ones. Home safely from the war and still strong in their beliefs, they were eager to return to their studies and begin a new life.

However, they saw that the old seminary had fallen into disrepair.

"We are strong, Joseph," Georg said. "We can work on restoring the old buildings."

"You're right," answered his brother. "We'll find some of our other friends and they'll be glad to help us."

In a short time, they were able to get together a team of workers and they began the difficult task.

Another problem to be faced was obtaining the proper reading material for the students. Even though no one could buy books in this desolate country, Joseph and Georg were able to borrow some from various pastors.

Within months, the building was repaired and books were ready. Philosophy and theology classes could then start. The students could return to the seminary where the two brothers would now be classmates.

They searched for the other seminarians with whom they had shared their lives before. Sadly, they learned that the war had taken many of their friends and left many others seriously injured. Grateful to be alive, the ones like Joseph and Georg who had been spared were eager to start again with hope for the future.

Although the seminary building was still being used as a military hospital, in November 1945 the school opened in a few vacant rooms. Most of the students were older men who had suffered the terror of the war for many years. At first they looked down on these young boys who had not gone through all the suffering they had, and wondered if they would be good priests. Gradually, though, a common bond developed as they all shared a hunger for knowledge and a desire to serve the Church.

Joseph and his brother spent two years in the study of philosophy in Freising. Then Joseph transferred to Munich University, which was almost in ruins. Living conditions were uncomfortable. Still, the learning environment and the lectures by famous professors made it all worthwhile.

After four hard years of study, the students were ready to go out into the world. They had learned their lessons and they had strengthened their love for God through daily Mass, prayers, and retreats. They were prepared to work, and they were ready to preach, say Mass, and give counsel.

June 19, 1951 was sunny and beautiful outside, and Joseph was excited about this day that would change his life. The beautiful cathedral in Freising was festive with flowers and bright candles. Every pew was crowded with loved ones. Sweet music and choir voices filled the air.

Joseph's parents and sister arrived early. They seated themselves close to the altar, wanting to see their very own Georg and Joseph taking part in the many rituals of ordination—prostration, the laying on of hands, anointing of the hands, and the giving of the chalice and paten. This was a moment they had long awaited.

As each man's name was called by the bishop, the candidate responded "*Adsum,*" meaning "Here I am." It was Joseph's turn to reply, and his heart was beating fast.

During the laying on of hands, the archbishop and the other priests prayed to the Holy Spirit, asking the Spirit to come down upon the young men. As the archbishop laid hands on him, Joseph saw a little lark fly up from the high altar in the cathedral and burst out into song. To Joseph it was a sign. He was filled with joy. He felt God was saying, "This is good, Joseph; you are on the right way."

The archbishop ordained Joseph, his brother Georg, and thirty-eight other men as priests forever.

"Can you believe it?" Papa whispered to Mama, who was using her new white handkerchief to wipe her eyes. "It has finally happened. Our boys are priests!" She squeezed his hand and murmured, "Thank you, God."

The following week, the new Father Joseph said his first Holy Mass in his parish church of St. Oswald. His family again knelt in thanksgiving to God. All the villagers turned out proudly to pray with them. Afterward, Joseph and Georg were invited to bring "the first blessing" into people's homes, and even total strangers greeted them. Joseph's heart told him he was truly a priest!

On August 1, Joseph became an assistant pastor in the parish of the Precious Blood. His pastor, Father Blumschein, welcomed him and became his mentor. Sitting with the young man on the sofa in the rectory living room that first night, he smiled and patted Joseph on the back.

"My son, I am happy that you are here with me. I know you will be a good priest, and I will help you in any way I can. There are many things you must learn, but the most important thing is that a priest has to glow...."

Joseph thought about this as he daily observed this good man. He understood that he must have kindness and devotion to his duty at all times. As he saw his mentor die while bringing the sacraments to a dying person, he learned that a good priest always considers others before himself. With Father Blumschein as an example, Joseph performed his duties with love and soon had his own glow!

Although he enjoyed being a parish priest and working with the people, especially the young ones, after a year he was ordered to resume his studies. His parents had another proud moment when, in July 1953, he walked across the stage and received the cap as doctor of theology.

CHAPTER 8

GOOD-BYES

◆◆◆

I t was 1955. Joseph's parents were getting old. His father was seventy-eight and his mother seventy-one. They still lived in their country home on the edge of the forest, where there were huge amounts of snow and the roads were frozen in the winter. Even in pleasant weather, the church and the shops were two kilometers (1.24 miles) away—a long walk for two older people.

One day when they were all together having supper, Joseph told them, "Papa, Mama, this is all too much for you. I know you don't want to move from your cozy home, but we have a plan. Wait till you hear it. I think you will be pleased."

It turned out that Joseph was lecturing at the university and was assigned to a house near the cathedral in Freising. It was perfect. The shops and church would be close by and the family would be together again. So on a foggy November day, before the snow had fallen, Joseph and Maria moved to the new place. Mama liked it so much that she immediately put on her apron and cooked up a feast.

When Christmas came, Joseph and Maria joyfully prayed at Midnight Mass with their daughter and two sons. They couldn't stop smiling. This strange new place had become their home.

After three years, Joseph was invited to take a position to teach in Bonn. It was like a dream come true, but he was worried about his parents since the house they now loved would no longer be available to them. This would have been a dilemma, if God's loving care had not at the same time provided Georg with a position as choir director back in their home parish of St. Oswald. There, he had the use of a little house in the middle of the city.

Joseph and his brother discussed the matter and spoke to their father.

"Oh, boys, I hate to move again," replied Mr. Ratzinger. "Mama likes it so much here. I know we will have to do it, though. Don't worry, I will break the news to her gently. She will understand."

Mama was disappointed, but she said, "I am proud of Joseph and know it is best for him. We'll be all right, and it will be nice to be back home again in our old village." So once again they packed up their furniture and prepared to move.

One hot day in August, Papa was carrying his daughter's typewriter to the repair shop when he had a mild stroke. The doctor examined him and he seemed to be all right.

"There's nothing to be concerned about right now. I'll just keep an eye on him," said the doctor.

When Christmas came, Papa gave his family special gifts. It was almost as though he knew it would be his last Christmas, but to his family, everything seemed fine for months.

The following August, Papa and Mama took a 10 kilometer (6.21 mile) walk, holding hands as they visited the old places where they had lived, chatting with friends, then stopping at church for a visit. When they reached home, Papa said, "Maria, I don't feel well. I hope the children get home soon. I am very tired."

"Just sit down for a bit, dear. I'll get dinner ready," Mama replied as she moved toward the kitchen.

She sang as she prepared the meat and fresh garden vegetables. A short time later, Joseph, Georg, and Maria walked in the door, filled with talk about their ride to Tittmoning that day.

Joseph dashed into the kitchen, hungry for his supper. He kissed his mother as he lifted a pot lid.

"Mama, that smells good. What are we having?" he asked.

"You'll see in a minute," she said as she called the others to the table.

They were about to sit down when Papa slowly got up from his chair in the parlor. Instead of joining them at the table, he opened the door and went outside, where he collapsed on the stone step. They ran to him.

"Papa, are you okay?" asked Georg as they lifted him up and brought him to his bed.

They called the doctor, who came quickly to the house. After an examination, he took off his stethoscope and put his arm around the mother.

"I am sorry, Mrs. Ratzinger, Joseph has had a serious stroke this time. I'm afraid he is not going to make it." Turning to the children, he added, "Take care of your mother. It won't be long."

Mama felt helpless as she sat down by the bed. She kept rubbing her husband's arm as tears poured down her cheeks. "Joseph, Joseph..." she cried. Raising her eyes to Heaven, she prayed, "God, please help us." Her husband couldn't speak, but his eyes spoke of his love for his wife.

Joseph, Georg, and Maria sat by the side of the bed. They whispered to their father, their voices choking, their eyes filled with tears.

Two days later, holy candles were lit as Mr. Ratzinger's sons, with oil and holy water, gave him the last sacraments. He gazed at the crucifix on the wall, smiled at them, and closed his eyes for the last time.

Joseph felt empty. His papa was gone. He wrapped his arms around his mother. Together they wept.

Five years later, another tragedy entered Joseph's life. In January, Georg called him, worried because their mother was not eating. They watched over her, encouraging her with her favorite foods. She seemed to be feeling better, but seven months later, her doctor summoned them to his office and told them, "Your mother has cancer of the stomach. I'm afraid I can't do anything for her. There is no further treatment... I will pray for her—and for you."

But Mama was not one to give up. Even though she was very frail, she continued to cook and keep house for Georg as if nothing were wrong.

One day in October while at a little shop in the village picking up meat for dinner, she collapsed. Her sons were called. They took her home where she went to bed, too weak to get up again. For weeks she was in constant pain, but she never complained. Then on December 16, 1963, her children knew the end was near.

They sat in the dark room, lit only by candles which burned low after her boys had anointed her with the oil of the sick. She held her beloved rosary and they prayed together. As they held her close, she closed her eyes and died.

Joseph knelt by her bedside as long as he could.

"She is with Papa now, but how can we live without her?" he asked his brother, as tears flowed down his cheeks.

As he wiped his own eyes, Georg agreed, "There's no one like our Mama...."

Joseph sat on the sofa, put his arm around his weeping sister, covered his eyes, and cried.

CHAPTER 9

BUSY YEARS

◆ ◆ ◆

During the years between his parents' deaths and for years afterwards, Joseph continued teaching and lecturing at the great German universities. For a while, he lived in Rome where he contributed his knowledge to Pope John XXIII's Vatican Council.

During this time, Joseph always stayed close to his brother and sister. They still spent much time together. In Regensburg, where he spent several years teaching, lecturing, and learning, he shared a little house complete with a garden with his sister, who was his secretary and friend. Often Georg, who was now a renowned choir director, was able to visit, and the three gathered together as a family.

This could not last, as Joseph became well-known as a theologian and was called to greater things in the Church. In 1976, he was handed a letter from Pope Paul VI, who asked him to accept an appointment as archbishop of Munich and Freising. Joseph shook his head as he read the words.

"I must pray over this and speak with my confessor," he told the papal representative. "I don't feel I'm qualified or prepared for such a position as this."

"Just think it over and get back to me with your decision," he was told.

That night Joseph had dinner with his friend, Father Auer, who was also his confessor. He told him the news. After Joseph read the letter aloud, he placed it on the table and looked at his friend.

"Johann, I know you will agree with me. I am not suited for this."

Father Johann cocked his head and smiled. "Joseph," he answered, "you must accept."

And so on a beautiful day in early summer, May 28, 1977, the cathedral in Munich, though still greatly damaged by the Allied bombs, radiated with colorful flowers, candles and a spirit of joy. Georg and Maria proudly watched as Joseph was anointed as Archbishop Ratzinger.

That evening Joseph, still a quiet young man, told his brother and sister, "I still can't believe that I have been chosen as a 'bearer of the Mystery of Christ.'"

Maria hugged him. "Joseph, we are so proud of you...and wouldn't Mama and Papa be so happy today if they were here with us! If only they were here," she said as she held the hands of her "little brother."

Georg smiled his agreement as he patted his brother on the back.

A few days later came another surprise. The pope had chosen five new cardinals—and one of them was Joseph Ratzinger! On June 27, 1977, Pope Paul VI made him a cardinal!

Soon afterwards, Joseph was invited to have a private audience with the pope. He admitted to the Holy Father that his natural shyness and unfamiliarity with the highest reaches of the Church left him uncertain in his actions.

"Joseph, don't worry, I know what I am doing. I have prayed about this and you are my choice. I'm happy with my decision. Now let us have some lunch — and talk about the weather," replied the pope.

As his episcopal motto, the new cardinal selected the phrase from the Third Letter of John, "Co-workers of the Truth." He felt it was a connection between his previous life as teacher and his new mission. At the time, Joseph could never have dreamt what his future mission would be!

Just over a year later, the pope died at age 81 after fifteen years as the Holy Father. Joseph, along with all the other cardinals, traveled to Rome to choose a new Pope. Albino Luciani was elected and took the name John Paul I — and they all flew back to their homes, content with their choice and prepared for a long reign. Joseph resumed his duties in Munich and Freising.

Only a month later, at the end of September while on a visit with the bishop of Quito, Ecuador, Joseph had gone to bed and was sound asleep when suddenly the room was filled with bright light. A priest entered the room and announced, "I am sorry to awaken you, Your Eminence, but it is my sad duty to tell you that the pope has died!"

This new cardinal, aware of what that meant, jumped out of bed and was soon on his way back to Rome. This time, Karol Wojtyla from Poland was selected and chose the name John Paul II.

Pope John Paul respected Joseph's intelligence as a theologian, and soon after the election he asked Joseph to be his prefect of the Congregation for Catholic Education. Joseph refused, as he felt he was not ready for this.

Three years later, the pope asked him to be prefect of the Congregation for the Doctrine of the Faith. This time, Joseph accepted.

For over 24 years Joseph held one of the most challenging and demanding positions in the Church —and it was not easy. He considered it his most uncomfortable post. He had to deal with the Church's most difficult problems — heresies, unacceptable theologies, difficult theologians, discipline, and other serious problems.

Due to the nature of this work and his innate shyness, Joseph became the object of controversy, of scorn, and of malicious misrepresentations. He was nicknamed "God's Rottweiler," "Inquisitor," and other cruel names. He was called a tyrant and a hated enemy of progress in the Church. Joseph was none of these. Closing his ears to all this, he persevered as he had been taught many years before by his father, silently bearing the burden he had accepted.

Pope John Paul realized that this shy scholarly man was a more accomplished theologian than he himself was. The two were a team who collaborated on all matters of importance facing the Church. They met in private every Friday night to discuss the business of the CDE and shared luncheons on Tuesday with the assistants who worked with them. Throughout the long years, though Cardinal Ratzinger was criticized, the pope remained firmly beside him.

While those who didn't really know the cardinal were disapproving of him, others saw a different, soft-hearted man. They saw a man who found it impossible to ignore the softest *meow* near his feet as he walked through Rome's parks filled with stray cats. He would always stop conversing and lean down to pet the little creatures who came to meet him. Sometimes he would pull from his pocket a little treat he had saved from his lunch to surprise them. He loved cats, and although he had no pet of his own, when he went home to Regensburg, the gardener's tabby was his best friend.

He was famous for walking the streets of Rome in a plain black cassock. Tourists mistook him for a simple priest. They stopped him to ask directions, what time Masses were held, and other questions. The few who recognized him were greeted with a smile.

Seminarians did know him and stopped to converse with him as he headed to work, briefcase in hand, a professor's beret on his head. He loved talking with them and always remembered their names, home countries, and even what the students were studying. He always had thanks for those who helped him in any way, regardless of their importance. Joseph was kind to everyone. Toward the end of his own life, Pope John Paul II spoke of Joseph as "my trusted friend."

By 1990 Joseph was ready to retire. The pope said, "My friend, we're both getting old. We must continue to work together."

Joseph again wanted to step down in 1991, 1996 and 2000, hoping to return to his writing and study. But this was not to be and never will be for him…now.

…On April 2, 2005, Pope John Paul II died.

CHAPTER 10

HABEMUS PAPAM

◆ ◆ ◆

On April 18, 2005, 115 members of the College of Cardinals gathered together to choose the successor to Pope John Paul II. That morning, Joseph, who was the Dean of Cardinals, prayed with them, "Let us go and pray to the Lord to help us bear fruit that endures...."

The next evening at 5:50 p.m., after four ballots, God answered that prayer. The huge crowd who had gathered in St. Peter's Square saw the white smoke billow into the sky and heard the bells of St. Peter's Basilica toll the news. The conclave was over—a new pope had been selected! The crowd waited anxiously, wondering who it would be.

Finally, the red velvet curtains parted on the balcony, and Cardinal Estevez walked to the balustrade and announced, "*Habemus papam!* I announce to you with great joy: We have a pope! The most eminent and most reverend...Joseph...Cardinal of the Holy Roman Church... Ratzinger...who has taken the name...Benedict XVI!"

The crowd burst into cheers and tears. The 78-year-old theologian, Joseph Aloysius Ratzinger, who had longed to return to his writing and studies, had become the 264th successor of Saint Peter. The curtains drew back once more, and Joseph, dressed in papal robes, walked forward and spoke to the people.

"Dear brothers and sisters, after the great Pope John Paul II, the cardinals have elected me, a simple and humble laborer in the vineyard of the Lord. The fact that the Lord knows how to work and to act even with inadequate instruments comforts me, and above all I entrust myself to your prayers.... The Lord will help us and Mary, His Most Holy Mother, will be at our side. Thank you."

Again the crowd roared as the new pope, with a smile, disappeared from their sight.

On Christmas Eve 2005, Pope Benedict urged people to spread joy through smiles and acts of kindness. "Joy is the true gift of Christmas, not expensive gifts," he said. Like Jesus, he urged us to love one another.

In his first encyclical, entitled *Deus Caritas Est* (God is Love), issued on January 25, 2006, he said, "Today, the term 'love' is the most frequently used and misused of words." He stressed selfless love for God and for one's neighbor. He told us that when we live in love, we live in God, and God lives in us.

We have a pope. We know his story. How it will end remains to be seen. We trust that this gentle, gracious, serene man of deep prayer and love of family and neighbor will lead us forward. Already he has begun his mission. Are we ready for ours?

May joy and love fill all our hearts!

CHOICE OF NAME
◆ ◆ ◆

"Filled with sentiments of awe and thanksgiving, I wish to speak why I chose the name Benedict. Firstly, I remember Pope Benedict XV, that courageous prophet of peace, who guided the Church through turbulent times of war. In his footsteps, I place my ministry in the service of reconciliation and harmony between peoples. Additionally, I recall Saint Benedict of Norcia, co-patron of Europe, whose life evokes the Christian roots of Europe. I ask him to help us all to hold firm to the centrality of Christ in our Christian life. May Christ always take first place in our thoughts and actions."

From his first General Audience in St. Peter's Square, April 27, 2005.

HIS OWN WORDS

"When you stand on the side of God, you do not necessarily stand on the side of success. Good fortune often seems to pamper precisely the cynics. How are we to understand this? The psalmist finds the answer by standing before God, in whose presence he grasps the ultimate insignificance of material wealth and success and recognizes what is truly necessary and what brings salvation."
—*Milestones: Memoirs*

"The vocation to love makes the human person an authentic image of God: Man and woman come to resemble God to the extent that they become loving people."
—June 6, 2006

"The Lord said, 'As often as you did it for one of my least brothers, you did it for me' (Matthew 25:40, 45). In every suffering person, especially if he or she is little and defenseless, it is Jesus who welcomes us and is expecting our love."
—September 30, 2006

"Faith cannot be reduced to a private sentiment or, indeed, be hidden when it is inconvenient; it also implies consistency and a witness even in the public arena for the sake of human beings, justice and truth."
—October 9, 2006

"God is not a relentless sovereign who condemns the guilty, but a loving father whom we must love, not for fear of punishment, but for his kindness, quick to forgive."
—October 19, 2006

"God loves everyone, because everyone is his creature. But some persons have closed their hearts…they think they do not need God, nor do they want him."

—December 25, 2006

"To be holy does not mean being superior to others; the saint can be very weak, with many mistakes in his life. Holiness is this profound contact with God, becoming a friend of God: it is letting the Other work, the Only One who can really make the world both good and happy."

—June 10, 2002

FURTHER READING

Benedict XVI. *Deus Caritas Est*. www.vatican.va.

Ratzinger, Joseph Cardinal. *Milestones—Memoirs: 1927-1977*. San Francisco, Ignatius Press, 1998.

Seewald, Peter. *Pope Benedict XVI: Servant of the Truth*. San Francisco, Ignatius Press, 2006.

CHRONOLOGY

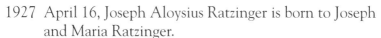

1927 April 16, Joseph Aloysius Ratzinger is born to Joseph and Maria Ratzinger.

1929 The Ratzinger family moves from Marktl am Inn to Tittmoning.

1937 The father, Joseph Ratzinger, retires from the police force and family moves to Hufschlag.

1939 September 1, World War II begins.
Young Joseph enters the minor seminary.

1941 Joseph, age 14, is forced to join Hitler Youth.

1943 Joseph is drafted into German army anti-aircraft corps.

1944 Joseph is released from anti-aircraft corps and in September receives draft notice into regular army.

1945 April 30, Adolph Hitler commits suicide.
In May, Joseph deserts the army and returns home. He is placed in prisoner-of-war camp.
June 19, Joseph returns home for good.
November, Joseph and Georg re-enter the seminary.

1946-1951 Joseph studies at University of Munich and at Freising.

1951 June 29, Joseph is ordained a priest.

1953 July, receives doctorate in theology.

1959 April 15, starts as full professor at University of Bonn.
August 23, Joseph's father dies.

1962 October 11, 1962, start of Second Vatican Council.
Joseph serves as advisor.

1963 December 16, Joseph's mother dies.

1977 March 24, named archbishop of Munich-Freising.
June 27, elevated to cardinal.

1981 November 25, becomes prefect of the Congregation for the Doctrine of the Faith.

1991 His sister Maria dies.

2002 November 30, elected dean of the College of Cardinals.

2005 April 2, Pope John Paul II dies.
April 19, Joseph elected as pope. He takes the name Benedict XVI.

GLOSSARY

◆ ◆ ◆

abide — dwell, remain.
ancestors — persons from whom one is descended.
anointing — pouring oil in a religious ceremony.
atrocities — cruel acts; wickedness.

balustrade — a row of posts topped by a rail.
barracks — a large building for lodging soldiers.
battalion — a body of troops.
bequeath — dispose of property by will.
billow — a surge like a sea wave.
blockade — a barring of entrance to and exit from a place,
        especially a port or coast.
brutally — cruelly.

cardinal — a member of the Catholic Church ranking just
        below the pope.
cassock — a priest's long garment.
ceremony — a rite on a formal occasion.
chalice — the cup which holds the Precious Blood during the
        Sacrifice of the Mass.
chancellor — the highest officer.
classical — referring to the literature of ancient Greece and
        Rome.
collaborated — worked with another.
conclave — a meeting of the cardinals for the election of the
        pope.
confessor — a priest who hears confession.
controversy — an argument.

desert — to leave without permission, not planning on return.
desolate — lonely; ravaged; abandoned.
dilemma — a choice between alternatives equally undesirable.
drafted — ordered to enter military service.
drill — military training, especially parade exercises.

eliminated — got rid of; removed.
eminent — high in rank or office.

environment — surrounding things or conditions.

episcopal — pertaining to a bishop.

executed — put to death according to law.

fervor — intense feeling.

forsake — abandon.

Führer — a German word meaning "leader."

generation — average difference in age from parent to child.

genetically — from heredity; from a family's physical background.

gymnasium — a secondary school preparing students for the university.

harsh — rough; severe.

hereditary — the transmission of characteristics from parent to child.

husky — hoarse; dry in the throat.

identified — recognized as an individual.

ideology — a set of beliefs, ideas, or doctrines.

illuminated — lit up.

initiation — induction to membership in a club.

insignia — a badge or emblem.

malicious — intending harm.

mandated — ordered by law.

mein — a German word meaning "my."

mentor — a trusted teacher.

ministry — the function of a clergyman.

motto — a word to express one's guiding principles.

Nativity — the birth of Christ.

National Socialism — the political beliefs of Hitler.

neckerchief — a scarf worn around the neck.

paten — the plate holding the Host at Mass.

pension — a regular paycheck for past services.

philosophy — a science dealing with general causes and principles of things.

political — pertaining to government.

progressive — advocating new methods.

prostrate — to lie flat or bow low.

providence — God's divine care.

rectory — home to priests.

regime — a rule of government.

regiment — a body of soldiers commanded by a colonel.

Reich — a German word meaning "empire."

reign — the time during which someone rules.

representative — an agent, a delegate, or a substitute.

resistance — opposing force.

reverend — a clergyman; one deserving respect.

rural — pertaining to country life.

SS troops — the most elite troops made up of only the best, racially pure Nazis.

savage — ferocious.

seminary — a school for men studying for the priesthood.

serene — calm.

Socialism — government ownership.

stamina — lasting strength; endurance.

stethoscope — an instrument for listening for sounds in the chest.

successor — one who follows or replaces another.

swastika — a form of a cross adopted as an emblem by the Nazi Party.

theology — the study of God and His divinity.

torture — to willfully inflict severe pain.

transports — method of moving troops from one place to another.

treason — violation against the state.

trenches — long narrow excavations in the ground as a shelter in warfare.

tyrant — an absolute ruler.

unison — together.

verbally — expressed in words.